6/1/94

To Wally
With best wishes
to a friend in Basking Ridge!

Walter Choroszewski

THE
GARDEN STATE
In Bloom

BY
WALTER CHOROSZEWSKI

INTRODUCTION BY
JOHN T. CUNNINGHAM

DEDICATION

In Loving Memory of Walter and Anna

A *garden is a lovesome thing, God wot!*
Rose plot,
Fringed pool,
Fern'd grot—
The veriest school
Of peace; and yet the fool
Contends that God is not—
Not God! in gardens! when the eve is cool?
Nay, but I have a sign;
'Tis very sure God walks in mine.
—Thomas Edward Brown (1663-1704)

T H E
GARDEN STATE
In Bloom

WALTER CHOROSZEWSKI

INTRODUCTION BY
JOHN T. CUNNINGHAM

Published by Aesthetic Press, Inc.
Somerville, NJ

DESIGNER
Walter Choroszewski

EDITORS
Walter and Susan Choroszewski

RESEARCH AND PRODUCTION ASSISTANT
Sherrie Bach

TYPESETTER
Martis Graphics, Edison, NJ

Printed and bound in Hong Kong

International Standard Book Number
0-933605-03-X

Library of Congress Catalog Card Number
92-97575

THE GARDEN STATE In Bloom

Published by
AESTHETIC PRESS, INC.
P.O. Box 5306, North Branch Station
Somerville, NJ 08876-1303

TITLE PAGE
Wetlands Institute Gardens, Stone Harbor, Cape May County

DEDICATION PAGE
Top Left: Rudolf W. van der Goot Rose Garden, Franklin Township, Somerset County
Top Right: Edith Duff Gwinn Memorial Garden, Barnegat Light, Ocean County
Bottom Left: Florence and Robert Zuck Arboretum at Drew University, Madison, Morris County
Bottom Right: Cross Estate Gardens, Bernardsville, Somerset County

INTRODUCTION

By

John T. Cunningham

New Jersey has been a floral wonderland for at least forty millennia, since the time when the last of the glaciers left behind a region where North met South botanically, a time when plants normally associated with the Carolinas met flora usually found only in the frozen lands of the Arctic Circle.

Thus, New Jersey's first settlers, the Lenape Indians, walked through great sprawling gardens set in place by nature. In springtime they trotted beneath flowering dogwood trees or trod on earthly blankets of violets. In summer, tall daisies nodded in the sunlight, and blue flag, the only natural iris in the state, flourished in meadows or swamps. Fall brought the asters and goldenrod.

Colonists appreciated the natural beauty, to the extent that very early propaganda, aimed at those still in Europe, called New Jersey "the Garden of America" as early as 1684. Adam Gordon, in a pamphlet written in 1765, reassured potential emigrants that New Jersey "very much resembles England."

The garden image has stuck: today New Jersey calls itself "The Garden State" and cynics wonder why. Highways, parking lots, and new developments seem to be everywhere, yet amid the concrete pavement and suburbia's weedless lawns, nature's garden shines through. Violets, daisies, asters, and goldenrod still flourish, handed down, seed by seed, through countless years and generations.

That natural beauty has been captured, often even enhanced, in scores, even hundreds, of known "formal" gardens in the state of New Jersey—formal in the sense that they are set aside, planned, planted, cared for, and opened to the public by individuals or groups of garden enthusiasts.

These gardens are Walter Choroszewski's focal point in his newest pictorial evidence of the things, natural and man-made, that make New Jersey unique. His photographs reflect the diversity and range of gardens that prosper everywhere, in urban parks beneath the shadows of tall buildings, as well as in the open reaches of southern New Jersey.

Defining a garden is not really possible. Are the blossoming cherry trees in Newark and Belleville's Branch Brook Park a garden? Are the long strips of tulips or chrysanthemums that brighten city parks or enhance suburban corporate acreage gardens? They meet a test of "formality," having been planned and perpetuated by humans.

Within these pages are gardens in state, county, and municipal parks, gardens that reflect the periods of historic houses, be they Colonial or Victorian; gardens that reflect pinpointed floral specialties, such as roses or irises; or gardens that define the words of a poet, such as the "Shakespeare Gardens" at the College of St. Elizabeth in Convent Station and Cedarbrook Park in Plainfield.

Tended areas outside the Tempe Wick House at Morristown, or the Johnson Ferry House at Washington Crossing, seek to recreate a garden reflecting a time when the farmer's wife would step out the door to select herbs and vegetables for the day's meal. Both reflect an era when a garden served both to beautify and to provide spices and herbs vital to life and comfort.

The influence of immigrants had altered for all time the floral nature of the Colonies. English housewives, eager for at least the fragrance and color of plantings at home, had brought seed for hollyhocks, Dutch wives had nurtured their tulips and daffodils across the ocean, and worldly sea captains had brought iris bulbs from their homelands. All of these are now as familiar in New Jersey's well-maintained gardens as are the natural violets of spring.

Understandably and properly, gardens usually display the selective passions of the planter. There is no finer example than the famed Presby Memorial Iris Garden in Upper Montclair, a breathtaking spread of 75,000 irises, arranged by variety, color, and historical connotations. Some of the rootstock dates back to the 16th century.

Theme gardens are popular and make sense. Leaming's Run Botanical Gardens in Cape May County features 27 separate gardens spread along a stream known as Leaming's Run. The viewer has a choice: colonial plants, ferns, herbs, bog flowers, evening bloomers, flowers by color, and an English cottage garden that befits the 1706 Thomas Leaming house, the only known dwelling remaining from Cape May's whaling days.

Contrastingly, yet in the same mode of theme gardens, the Duke Gardens near Somerville reaches around the world for inspiration—from the fine-honed quality of the patterned French Garden to the riotous color of the English border garden, from the lush mystery of the Chinese Garden to the simplicity and style of the Persian Garden. These gardens change with the four seasons, a luxury afforded because all are located under an acre of glass.

New Jersey's heritage, historical as well as botanical, is amply reflected throughout this book. Gardens continue to give us visual living clues of our ancestors and their lives in New Jersey.

The Barclay Farmstead in Cherry Hill takes inspiration from the longtime Quaker practicality and simple understatement in the southern part of the state. Quite the opposite, the Ringwood Manor gardens near the New York State border in Passaic County suggest America's age of opulence; when Mrs. Hewitt laid out her garden in 1895, she was influenced by the gardens at Versailles.

Arboretums, where trees and shrubs predominate in gardens of a larger scale, are found in almost every part of the state. In the main, they are legacies of well-to-do former owners who used time and money to create gardens that conformed with the owner's notions of landscaping and natural beauty.

The Golden Age of New Jersey's wealthy lives on through these gardens and arboretums. Estates are scattered throughout New Jersey—Frelinghuysen, Kuser, and Physick; many have special names—"Shadow Lawn," "Skylands," or "Glenmont." In recent years, most have become areas that are open to the public.

Nothing quite distinguishes New Jersey more than its diversity of terrain and soil types. These range from the mountains of the northwest to the 127 miles of seafront on the east and southeast, from the hardwood forests of the Highlands to the Pine Barrens of the south, from the glacial lake beds in the north to the sedgelands along the Delaware Bay.

The terrain accounts for the fact that considerably more than a thousand different wildflowers can be found within the state's boundaries. It accounts for the fact that wild orchids of the south grow side by side with the bearberry, a flowering plant normally associated only with the tundra of northern Canada.

Walter Choroszewski's penchant for natural beauty easily encompasses that diversity within these pages. The seashore, for example, is manifested in the Edith Duff Gwinn Garden at Barnegat Light and the Hereford Inlet Lighthouse Garden in North Wildwood—two gardens that might be overlooked by shore enthusiasts.

Gardens are meant to be seen, to be savored, to stroll through, and to be remembered by as many people as possible. Several New Jersey gardens have been designed for those whose senses are impaired or whose mobility is limited.

Two such user-friendly areas prove the point. The Fragrance and Sensory Garden in Somerset County's Colonial Park Arboretum gives sensitive awareness that flora can be enjoyed by smelling, touching, or eating; plants are chosen for those qualities. Similarly, Iselin's Garden for the Blind and Physically Impaired has added braille markers to the flowers and shrubs selected for sensory pleasures.

This book sparkles because of the quality and appropriateness of the photographic eye. Beyond that vital quality, however, it is an underscoring of New Jersey's historical and geographical contrasts.

The reader would be ill-served by a book on gardens that merely tantalized. The overwhelming thought on viewing a garden picture is the wish to see it. Leading people to a secret corner of the Pine Barrens in search of wild orchids would be a sin; not guiding them to these public gardens would be equally unthinkable.

Armchair enjoyment is possible in these pages but they are intended as well to provoke the viewer out of the chair and into the gardens. A directory with locations and telephone numbers is provided. If that suggests a guide, consider that a dividend.

Tiptoe through the tulips. . . . Stop to smell the roses. . . . Enjoy, then, this remarkable pictorial journey through New Jersey's gardens.

$\mathcal{C}$harles Smith Olden, whose family was among the earliest settlers of Princeton, built a Greek Revival mansion there in 1835. Olden, a gentleman farmer, became involved in politics as a state senator and was eventually elected governor. In 1893 the estate was sold to Moses Taylor Pine, a Princeton University trustee, who named the estate "Drumthwacket"—a Scottish term meaning "Wooded Hill." Abram Spanel, an inventor, became the third and final owner in 1941 until 1966, when the state of New Jersey purchased the property. The New Jersey Historical Society initiated a restoration plan, which was followed by the 1982 formation of the Drumthwacket Foundation to continue the plan and to serve as curator for this historic site.

Drumthwacket, Princeton, Mercer County

Drumthwacket now serves as New Jersey's official gubernatorial residence, with Governor and Mrs. James Florio becoming its first residents. Lucinda Florio, the governor's wife, took an active role in the rehabilitation of Drumthwacket's gardens. In 1991 she started a fund-raising campaign, consulted with experts from Cook College of Rutgers University and landscape professionals, and launched a multi-phase plan for the grounds. The new gardens at Drumthwacket are not a restoration of the original landscape plan, but rather a contemporary version which complements the original classic design. With its extended terrace and parterre, the new gardens were planned for "entertaining" to meet the social demands of a governor.

Drumthwacket, Princeton, Mercer County

On the grounds of New Jersey's State Capitol Complex, which overlooks the Delaware River, stately trees and numerous formal plantings complement this historic area. The main attraction of the Capitol Complex is the magnificent State House, which was basically rebuilt in 1885 after a fire destroyed the original 1792 structure. Between the State House and its neighboring Annex building, built in 1930, lies a spring oasis resplendent with flowering cherry trees and thousands of colorful tulips. Similar spring plantings bloom throughout Trenton's capitol district and are under the care of the state's Capitol Services.

New Jersey State Capitol Complex Gardens, Trenton, Mercer County

N amed "Skyland Farms," the original estate owned by Francis Lynde Stetson was elegant with its stylish mansion, lawns, and gardens, which were designed by the prominent landscape architect Samuel Parsons, Jr., around the turn of the century. Skylands was sold in 1922 as a summer home to Clarence McKenzie Lewis, who set out to make it a botanical showplace. For 30 years, Lewis collected plants from all over the world as well as from New Jersey roadsides, creating one of the finest collections in the state. In 1966 the state of New Jersey purchased Skylands Manor and Gardens as its first transaction under the new Green Acres program; in 1984 Governor Thomas H. Kean designated the central 96 acres as the state's official botanical garden, exhibiting a plethora of nearly 5,000 species and varieties of plants.

New Jersey State Botanical Gardens at Skylands, Ringwood, Passaic County

Lewis stressed symmetry, color, texture, form, and fragrance in creating his gardens, which were designed for the senses. Changing color is found in the original designs of the Annual Garden and nearby Perennial Border. Spring offers specialized areas of interest such as the Lilac Garden, Magnolia Walk, Azalea Garden, Rhododendron Display Garden, and the striking Crab Apple Vista. Through the remainder of the year a variety of other formal gardens, terraces, statuary, and informal plantings provide much visual interest. The gardens are maintained by the state's Division of Parks and Forestry, with strong support through fund raising and volunteerism by the Skylands Association.

etween the stately Greenfield Hall and the historic Samuel Mickle House in Haddonfield lies a small herb garden reminiscent of Colonial times. The garden is part of the property of the Historical Society of Haddonfield, a site which dates to 1732. Greenfield Hall, a Classic Revival mansion built in 1841, is headquarters for the society; the 1736 Samuel Mickle House was moved to the society's property in 1965. The herb garden was established in 1976 by the Haddonfield Garden Club and features a central beehive surrounded by a variety of culinary and medicinal herbs, each identified by a ceramic marker.

As the last wartime headquarters of General George Washington, Rockingham is the house where Washington delivered his farewell address to the troops on November 7, 1783. In this 20-room farmhouse, built in the 1730s, Washington also entertained important guests, including Thomas Jefferson, James Madison, and Alexander Hamilton. Rockingham was part of a large Colonial plantation, and the house has survived several moves. In the 1960s the Stoney Brook Garden Club of Princeton designed and planted, and continues to maintain, a re-creation of an 18th-century herb garden at Rockingham. Authentic Colonial plantings add to the charm of this state historic site near Rocky Hill.

Rockingham Herb Garden, Franklin Township, Somerset County

*I*n the 1740s Dirck Dey built his Georgian manor house in the Preakness Valley of Passaic County. His son, Theunis Dey, served in the Revolution as colonel of the Bergen County Militia, where his position brought him in constant communication with General George Washington. In July of 1780 the Dey Mansion served as Washington's headquarters while his troops were camped in the valley. The estate was purchased in 1930 by the Passaic County Parks Commission, and after some restoration it was opened as a museum in 1934. The grounds contain a formal garden, an herb and vegetable garden, and a knot garden which was created in cooperation with the Riverview Garden Club and the Eagle Scouts Troop 134 of Wayne Township.

*P*rospect House, a Florentine-style mansion built in 1849, was once the residence of Princeton University's presidents. At the rear of the house a flower garden was developed in 1904 by Ellen Wilson, after her husband, Woodrow Wilson, installed a fence around the grounds to reduce student traffic. A curtain of hemlocks and evergreens serves as a backdrop for this semicircular garden which is ablaze with color in spring, summer, and fall. Tulips, daffodils, and hyacinths start the season, followed by brightly hued midsummer annuals and perennials, with chrysanthemums adding color in the autumn. In addition to the flowers, numerous specimen trees and shrubs, both native and exotic, complete the scene at Prospect Gardens.

Prospect Gardens at Princeton University, Princeton, Mercer County

uilt in 1796, the house of Israel Crane, a merchant in Montclair, had many owners before the YWCA purchased it in 1920. In 1965, the Montclair Historical Society, which was formed to preserve this building, moved the house to its present site on Orange Road. In 1974, the 1818 home of Nathanial Crane was added to the property, and restored in the style of a "General Store." Between the houses, the museum grounds are beautified with a variety of formal plantings—a professionally designed Colonial herb garden, vegetable garden, and various beds of straw-type annuals and perennials used for drying and for crafts.

Crane House Museum Garden, Montclair, Essex County

*F*armed during the 18th and 19th centuries until its fall to a sheriff's lien in 1890, the property known today as Deep Cut Gardens was sold for taxes in 1907. It remained undeveloped until 1935, when Vito Genovese purchased the property, renovated the old farmhouse, and constructed gardens of Italian and English style. Subsequent owners, the Cubbages and Wihtols, cared for the gardens until Mrs. Wihtol's death in 1977, when the 20 acres were donated to the Monmouth County Park System. Expanded to 53 acres, the park features a Horticultural Center and a diversity of garden areas, including a rockery, parterre, pergola, shade garden, and greenhouses.

Deep Cut Gardens, Middletown, Monmouth County

*H*ezekiah B. Smith, an inventor and manufacturer from Lowell, Massachusetts, purchased the nearly deserted mill town of Shreveville for $23,000 and turned it into a national industrial complex, renamed Smithville. The H.B. Smith Company manufactured 150 different styles of machines and held patents for 30 inventions. Smith eventually turned his attention to the 1840 Greek Revival mansion and made numerous changes, such as encircling the mansion with a brick-and-stone wall surmounted by cast-iron pickets and creating an extensive boxwood garden and glass conservatory. Today, Smithville lives on as Burlington County's first park; the restored mansion complex and gardens are under the care of the County Cultural and Heritage Department and volunteers of Friends of the Mansion at Smithville.

Smithville Mansion Courtyard Gardens, Eastampton Township, Burlington County

A ngelsea was a fishing village with a light-house on the northern point of a Cape May County barrier island. This area is known today as North Wildwood. Since 1986, the grounds and gardens surrounding the Victorian Hereford Inlet Lighthouse have been steadily improved by the North Wildwood Parks Department, with plantings of trees, shrubs, flowers, and ornamental grasses. The new plants feature a mixture of native and non-native species which are salt-tolerant. Designs of the flower beds are based on cottage gardens and elements of Victorian gardens that reflect the late 19th-century period of the lighthouse.

Hereford Inlet Lighthouse Gardens, North Wildwood, Cape May County

A Victorian era garden restoration, initiated by the Home Garden Club of Morristown, surrounds the Italianate Victorian mansion, Acorn Hall—home to the Morris County Historical Society. John Schermerhorn was the first owner, selling it to Augustus Crane, whose family occupied the house for 114 years before Mary Crane Hone donated the estate to the Historical Society in 1971. Only plant materials available to the original gardeners were used in the restoration. In early spring, a gazebo decorated with cast iron bands of oak leaves and acorns serves as a focal point from which to view the many exotic flowering trees, shrubs, bulbs, and perennials that surround the open lawn. A magnificent red oak on the front lawn is the reason for the name given to this 1853 estate home.

A prosperous Dutch shipping settlement, known in the early 1700s as Raritan Landing, is better known today as Johnson Park in Piscataway. It is here that the Middlesex County Cultural and Heritage Commission maintains East Jersey Olde Towne, a 12-acre site filled with original Colonial and replica structures obtained throughout the county, including a school, church, tavern, and homes. Behind Dr. Vanderveer's home and office is a charming herb garden enclosed by a white fence. A brick pathway leads through sections of medicinal and culinary herbs that were common in the Colonial period. A volunteer effort at East Jersey Olde Towne is responsible for the loving care of this garden.

East Jersey Olde Towne Herb Garden, Piscataway, Middlesex County

*H*ardscrabble House, built in 1905, was part of the "Mountain Colony" that developed in the Bernardsville hills as a summer retreat for wealthy New York executives. It was sold in 1929 to W. Redmond Cross and Julia Newbold Cross. As a member of the Royal Horticultural Society, Julia Cross commissioned the noted landscape architect Clarence Fowler to develop an English country garden and pergola. Mrs. Cross continued to cultivate her gardens until her death in 1972; three years later the estate was added to the Morristown National Historic Park. After years of neglect, a volunteer effort was launched to restore the gardens, which are currently maintained by the New Jersey Historical Garden Foundation in cooperation with the National Park Service.

Cross Estate Gardens, Bernardsville, Somerset County

A bram Garris operated a grist mill along Van Campens Brook in 1832. Within a few years, a general store and blacksmith shop were built near the mill, and other tradesmen also opened businesses nearby, thus creating the village of Millbrook. As technology, railroads, and competition passed it by in the late 1800s, the village was no longer a bustling center of commerce. Today, Millbrook is alive again as a restoration 19th-century rural community, part of the Delaware Water Gap National Recreation Area. Within the village there is a garden containing a representation of the crops of the 19th century—fruit trees and vegetables, including corn, beans, and squash, as well as one of the leading cash crops of the time, tobacco!

Millbrook Village Garden, Millbrook, Warren County

*C*yrus Hyde's lifelong interest in herbs began during his childhood in Totowa, where he and his mother would search the local woodlands for medicinal herbs. In 1967 Cyrus and his wife Louise purchased a home in the rolling hills of Warren County on four and one-half acres of poor, rocky soil. Over the next 26 years the Hydes designed, developed, and are still the proprietors of a garden and nursery that specializes in all types of herbs. The formal gardens include numerous varieties of geranium, rosemary, basil, and thyme; a traditional knot garden was created from barberry, hyssop, and lavender. In addition to the formal areas, the nursery's fields of herbs add to the color of the landscape.

𝒥 ce-age artistry from
the Wisconsin Glacier
left Leonard J. Buck
with a pond, stream, and some
unusual rock outcroppings on
his Far Hills property. As a
mining engineer, Buck was
fascinated by the potential of
this site. In the late 1930s he
met with Zenon Schreiber,
noted rock garden designer,
and together they developed
the valley with native and
exotic plantings, creating a
spectacular alpine rock garden.
In 1950 Buck received the
Gold Medal of the National
Association of Gardeners for
his efforts in this transformation. Buck and Schreiber
continued to develop the garden
until Leonard J. Buck's death
in 1974.

The Somerset County Park Commission became the new caretaker of the garden after Helen Buck donated the site to the county in 1976. Heaths, heathers, ferns, rock-loving plants, and wildflowers share this woodland stream valley with dogwoods, azaleas, and rhododendron. In 1986 the garden also added the exceptional F. Gordon Foster Hardy Fern Collection, from Sparta, New Jersey, further enhancing the diverse assortment of plants found at Buck Gardens. This maturing garden is ecologically sound, and gives the appearance of being untouched by human hands.

*H*istory comes alive at the Longstreet Farm, where a reproduction of a family farm provides us a glimpse of late-19th-century rural life. Hendrick Longstreet inherited this farm from his grandfather in 1806 and it remained as the Longstreet homestead for more than a century. Subsequent family heirs eventually sold the farm to Monmouth County in 1967. The county opened it to the public in 1972, and 11 years later created the Longstreet Farm living history site. In addition to the popular farm animals, Longstreet Farm also offers a kitchen garden and cutting garden featuring heirloom varieties of flowers and vegetables that were locally available to the Longstreets. The gardens are under the care of the Longstreet Farm staff, aided by volunteers.

Longstreet Farm, Holmdel Township, Monmouth County

*M*ilton Erlanger was a benefactor and trustee of Monmouth College, and the gardens outside Wilson Hall are named in his memory. Long Branch was a shore resort famous for being visited by several presidents; on this site was the summer home of President Woodrow Wilson. The Wilson manse burned down in 1927, and a new mansion, styled after Versailles, was built two years later by the new owner, H.T. Parson, then president of F.W. Woolworth Co. The estate, known as "Shadow Lawn" for the magnificent shade trees that bordered the lawns, also featured numerous vegetable gardens, flower gardens, berry patches, and grape arbors. Parson hired Achille Duchêne of Paris to design the formal terrace garden just west of the mansion. Duchêne used a colonnade design to create a peristyle "teahouse" and "water organ" with fountains, also adapted from the gardens at Versailles.

Erlanger Memorial Gardens at Monmouth College, West Long Branch, Monmouth County

George Perot Macculloch, a Scotsman born in Bombay and educated in Edinburgh, came to America in 1806, and was best known for his conception, planning, and building of the Morris Canal. In 1810 he built a red brick Federal-style mansion in Morristown that remained the Macculloch homestead for 139 years. The estate was purchased in 1949 by W. Parsons Todd, who restored the mansion and gardens and opened them to the public as a museum. The gardens were restored by the Garden Club of Morristown, and feature seasonal plantings, a collection of old-fashioned roses, and a wisteria trellis with rootstock brought from Japan by Commodore Matthew C. Perry.

Macculloch Hall Gardens, Morristown, Morris County

       n 1888, Fred Kuser bought the Benjamin Goldy Farm to build a summer "Country Place"—a 22-room, Queen Anne–style mansion completed in 1892. For more than 30 years, the Kuser family would move from their home in New York to spend the summer months in the country, before making it their permanent residence in 1926. During this time, formal Victorian gardens surrounded the mansion, and were embellished with a gazebo, marble benches, and peacocks strutting across the lawns. The estate remained as the Kuser homestead until 1976, when it was purchased by Hamilton Township with the assistance of Green Acres funding, and opened as a park the following year. Today there are numerous flowering shrubs, formal plantings of annuals and perennials, and a gazebo to remind us of its Victorian grandeur.

Kuser Farm Mansion Gardens, Hamilton Township, Mercer County

*H*istoric Phoenix House, originally built as an academy, became a popular 19th-century hotel and tavern in the center of the summer resort town of Mendham. After its halcyon days as a famous inn, Phoenix House later became a tearoom, antique shop, and dress shop, until finally in 1938 it was turned over to the Borough of Mendham "for the good of the community." The adjacent lot fell into neglect until a group of women formed the Mendham Garden Club to beautify the plot. Martha Brookes Hutcheson, the noted landscape architect, designed the garden for the club in an early 19th-century style, with an oval walkway around a central lawn, and a perennial garden with numerous trees and shrubs. For over 50 years, the maintenance of this garden has been the focus of the Mendham Garden Club.

Phoenix House Garden, Mendham, Morris County

*N*ear the shadows of Barnegat Lighthouse, the Barnegat Light Historical Society maintains a small museum, and on its grounds is found a garden named in honor of its co-founder, Edith Gwinn, who, with Frances Selover, initiated the garden project from a "weedy lot" in 1962. In the 1980s the Long Beach Island Garden Club joined the museum garden project, creating a lush oasis near the beach. A winding path weaves through this compact garden of colorful annuals, perennials, and shrubs, featuring many shore-oriented plants, all offering abundant summer color near the shore.

Edith Duff Gwinn Memorial Garden, Barnegat Light, Ocean County

R ingwood Manor, an ironmaster's estate since 1740, has been home to three families since the Revolution, when it was also used as headquarters for General George Washington. The Hewitts were the third family to occupy this grand mansion, and Mrs. Hewitt was

*P*rinceton's Marquand Park is unique in its history of owners who were all avid horticulturists and collectors of rare plant specimens, making it a living museum of trees and shrubs from around the world, including eight of the largest trees of their species recorded in New Jersey. The park began as a 30-acre farm purchased in 1842 by a Princeton University professor, who entrusted the design to the world-renowned gardener, Mr. Petrey, with subsequent owners embellishing on the original plan. The Marquand family was the final owner before its heirs donated 17 acres to the borough of Princeton for use as a public park. Marquand Park is maintained as an arboretum by the Borough of Princeton in cooperation with the Marquand Park Foundation.

Marquand Park, Princeton, Mercer County

At the Tempe Wick House in the Jockey Hollow section of Morristown National Historic Park, the Wick House Kitchen Garden is maintained as a demonstration garden for educational and living history purposes. A wide array of 18th-century herbs for culinary, domestic, and medicinal uses, as well as vegetables and fruit trees which were common to northern New Jersey during Colonial times, are grown on the original garden site. It is cared for by the National Park Service in cooperation with the Northern New Jersey Unit of the Herb Society of America.

Wick House Kitchen Garden, Harding Township, Morris County

$\mathcal{L}$enni-Lenape Indians once gathered at the open fields, springs, and large rock shelter of today's Brookdale Park. In the 17th century, Dutch settlers changed the area into farm fields and grazing land, and it became known as Stonehouse Plains. By the late 1800s, a new post office had renamed the area Brookdale. Essex County began purchasing land in 1928 for the creation of Brookdale Park, which was completed in 1937. Designed by the renowned Olmsted Brothers, the park was intended to be a type of arboretum with many of the native species being replaced by exotic trees and shrubs. Complementing the Olmsted plan, the North Jersey Rose Society donated 750 rose bushes in 1959 for the creation of a rose garden, which is today maintained by the Essex County Parks Department.

Brookdale Park Rose Garden, Bloomfield and Montclair, Essex County

*A*ndover Forge was a key supplier of armaments to the Continental Army during the Revolution. Renamed Waterloo in the early 19th century, the village continued to grow with the opening of the Morris Canal in 1831. Waterloo prospered through the Victorian era, after which a gradual decline was caused by the railroad bypassing the village. In the 1940s, Percival H.E. Leach and Louis D. Gualandi initiated the revival of the village, which first opened to tourists in 1964. Thanks to their lifelong efforts, Waterloo now operates as a restoration village with more than 28 buildings. Colonial and Victorian plantings are found throughout the village; however, an herb garden, designed and planted by Cyrus Hyde, is especially noteworthy. Near the herb garden a memorial well honors co-founder Louis D. Gualandi. The gardens and village are cared for by the Waterloo Foundation for the Arts.

*C*aroline Bamberger Fuld was impressed with the flowering cherry trees she saw in Washington, D.C. In 1927 this avid gardener and philanthropist offered to donate over 2,000 trees to the Essex County Park system. As she had planned, this gift display of flowering cherry trees in Branch Brook Park, the largest display in America, has become a New Jersey natural landmark. Since the original gift, Essex County has added more than 1,500 new trees, boasting a total of more than 3,000, including 28 varieties of single blossom, double blossom, and weeping cherry trees. This total greatly surpasses, in number and variety, the trees around the Tidal Basin in Washington, D.C. Each April thousands of visitors pass through the park to enjoy this spectacle of spring.

Branch Brook Park, Newark and Belleville, Essex County

*W*ithin the suburban residential neighborhood of Short Hills lies a 16-acre preserve started in 1923 by Cora Louise Hartshorn, daughter of Stewart Hartshorn, the founder of the town. "Miss Cora" was an artist and naturalist, and upon her death in 1958 the arboretum was bequeathed to Millburn Township, which maintains the preserve in conjunction with a volunteer-based association. Three miles of hiking trails traverse this glacial moraine. In spring, mountain laurel, azaleas, and rhododendrons color the hillsides; in fall, brilliant foliage illuminates the deciduous woodland oasis. Near Stone House, the visitors center, a wildflower garden provides continuous bloom from spring through the first frost.

Cora Hartshorn Arboretum, Short Hills, Essex County

$\mathcal{E}$stablished in 1963, Holmdel Arboretum's 20-acre site abounds with hundreds of species of cultivars and a wide variety of ornamental trees and shrubs. Flowering crab apples, cherries, and plums color the hillside in spring. Contributions of specimens by the nurserymen of the county as well as numerous other memorial plantings have provided the arboretum with a strong base of trees, shrubs, and woody plants that thrive in Monmouth County. The arboretum is maintained by the Monmouth County Shade Tree Commission in cooperation with the Monmouth County Park System.

Holmdel Arboretum, Holmdel Township, Monmouth County

*D*uke Farms was the 2,500-acre country estate of James Buchanan Duke, tobacco and utilities magnate. J.B. Duke's interest in orchids was the inspiration for his building of greenhouses on the estate. In 1912 he hired the architec[?] of Lord & Burnham to design and construct the glass structures. Duke Farms began to cultivate orchids and eventual[?] produced them commercially, along with a variety of other flowers which were supplied to the New York flower markets during the 1930s through the 1950s. With the advent of air freight and an abundant supply of flowers from around the world, Duke Farms' commercial flower production fell into decline, and plans were made to raze the greenhouses.

It was Doris Duke, J.B. Duke's daughter, who decided to convert the greenhouses into display gardens. In 1958 she personally designed and began the creation of Duke Gardens, a showcase of 11 thematic gardens from diverse cultures and regions of the world. Over the next few years she traversed the globe seeking ideas and specimens to complete her visionary gardens, which were opened to the public in 1964. English, French, Italian, Chinese, Japanese, and Indo-Persian designs are neighbors to semi-tropical, desert, and rain forest environments; meticulous in their presentation, all are "perfection under an acre of glass."

Duke Gardens, Hillsborough Township, Somerset County

*C*reated in 1932, the arboretum commemorates a historic area within Washington Crossing State Park, the site where General George Washington made his fateful crossing of the Delaware River on Christmas night of 1776. The arboretum was designed to feature the "common trees of New Jersey," but it is best known for the spring display of ornamental cherries, crab apples, and dogwoods that borders a great lawn and pathway just above the river. The arboretum lies within a short walk of the Johnson Ferry House and is cared for by the State of New Jersey's Division of Parks and Forestry.

George Washington Memorial Arboretum, Washington Crossing, Mercer County

*O*n the road to the mountains through the "West Fields of Elizabethtown," Samuel Miller built his brace-and-beam farmhouse in 1740. Joseph Cory acquired the property in 1784, and it remained in the Cory family until 1921. The Westfield Historical Society purchased the property in 1972 and created a living history museum, and it has since been maintained by the Miller-Cory House Association. The Millers and the Corys were rural farmers, and today's Miller-Cory House offers a variety of plantings including an herb garden with a quaint well house and a fine kitchen garden featuring only Colonial-era vegetables. Additional garden areas are dedicated to woodland flowers and shrubs, flax and dye plants, roadside wildflowers, berry bushes, and an orchard—all neatly positioned on three-quarters of an acre in Westfield.

Miller-Cory House Gardens, Westfield, Union County

William Trent, a native of Scotland, settled in Philadelphia around 1682, and became a successful merchant and shipowner. In 1714 he purchased land along the Assunpink Creek at the Falls of the Delaware, and five years later built a brick mansion there as his summer estate. With additional land purchases, he laid out a master plan for the site which he called "Trent's Town." After numerous residents since Trent, the last owner, Edward Ansley Stokes, donated the property to the city of Trenton in 1929 to be preserved as a historic house museum. The Garden Club of Trenton joined the project and began the restoration of the grounds in 1938, including the creation of a quadrangle herb garden around a sundial. The club's volunteer efforts in maintaining the grounds continue today in cooperation with the Trent House Association.

Trent House Herb Garden, Trenton, Mercer County

Established in 1974 as a joint effort of the Iselin Lions Club and the Woodbridge Garden Club, the garden was designed to serve the needs of the visually and physically handicapped. The "Circle of the Senses," with flowers and herbs awaiting one's touch, sits atop a waist-level planter with handrails and braille markers. Conveniently located along the parking area of the Iselin Library, the garden has no barriers, gates, or steps. This special garden, with its spectacular displays of annuals and perennials, and its rose garden, rock garden, and primrose path, is enjoyed by all in the community.

Garden for the Blind and Physically Handicapped, Iselin, Middlesex County

Mountainside Park in Upper Montclair is home to the world-renowned Presby Memorial Iris Garden, established in 1927 and named in honor of Frank H. Presby, founder of the American Iris Society. Featuring 75,000 irises, containing more than 6,000 varieties from around the world, Presby Iris Garden contains historic rootstock of European irises dating from the 1500s, with the addition of new hybrids each year. Although certain varieties may bloom from early spring to late fall, the spectacular peak of the bloom usually occurs near Memorial Day and lasts a few weeks. As a National Historic Landmark, the garden is jointly maintained by the Montclair Garden Club, Citizen's Committee of the Garden, and the Township of Montclair.

Presby Memorial Iris Garden, Upper Montclair, Essex County

 rew University's 186-acre wooded campus is a remnant of the original vast woodlands that covered New Jersey. Part of an Indian tract that was purchased in 1708 by the Gibbons family of Georgia, this forest was later purchased in 1866 by Daniel Drew to found a Theological School; in 1928 a College of Liberal Arts was created, followed by the addition of a Graduate School in 1955. Well aware of its natural forest asset, in 1980 Drew University created the Florence and Robert Zuck Arboretum adjacent to the Drew Forest Preserve. Formerly gardens of the Geraldine R. Dodge estate, the arboretum consists of nature trails that surround two ponds, serving as a natural laboratory for research and teaching botany. It is also home to migrating wildlife and a peaceful refuge for all who visit.

*W*hite House Farm, as it was known in the mid 1700s, sits high above the Raritan River in New Brunswick. According to local historians, George Washington stated that he loved the beautiful setting second only to his farm, Mount Vernon, on the Potomac. With lilac and cherry dating back over 200 years, the gardens are rich in history. Colonel Joseph Warren Scott purchased the farm in 1829 and renamed the estate "Buccleuch" in honor of his ancestor, the Duke of Buccleuch in Scotland. In 1911 heirs presented the mansion and 80 acres to the City of New Brunswick for use as a public park. The city restored and continues to maintain the gardens, which feature stately old boxwoods, roses, and geometric flower beds covered with more than 6,000 annuals.

Buccleuch Mansion Gardens, New Brunswick, Middlesex County

$\mathcal{L}$andscaping near the Cannonball Museum began in 1976 as a Bicentennial project sponsored by the Garden Club of Plainfield. Today, the site, which adjoins the Village Green in Scotch Plains, offers a variety of formal plantings, including a six-sided geometric garden with geraniums and boxwood, a culinary kitchen garden, and a grape arbor covering a brick pathway. A second area, the Marion Foster Loizeaux Memorial Garden, is an herb garden centered by an unusual primitive rock with a concave center, possibly once an Indian mortar stone. The rock now serves as a natural bath for the garden's avian visitors.

Arranged by separating the flower groups according to the plays, the Shakespeare Garden at the College of Saint Elizabeth offers a unique approach to a classic garden. Established in 1925, the gardens slowly developed through the late 1920s and culminated with the addition of a Carrara marble bust of Shakespeare in 1931. After years of neglect the gardens are finding new life under the current restoration project. The garden has a simple design of two intersecting pathways across a great lawn, each lined with defined plots for more than 20 of Shakespeare's major plays and poems, and displaying the flowers featured in each.

Shakespeare Garden at College of St. Elizabeth, Convent Station, Morris County

*B*ergen County was the site of many skirmishes in the Revolutionary War. In an area known today as Van Saun Park, a vigorous spring still flows; it was once used as a source of pure water for the American Continental Army. According to local legend, General George Washington drank from the spring while reviewing his troops. In the early 1960s, a garden was developed around the spring and is maintained by the Bergen County Department of Parks and Master Gardeners of Rutgers Cooperative Extension Service. Each April and May the garden comes alive with lush plantings of azaleas and rhododendrons. A charming footbridge crosses the brook, offering a special vantage point for viewing the colorful blossoms.

Washington Spring Garden at Van Saun Park, Paramus, Bergen County

*H*unterdon County, rural by nature, was slow in developing a park system; however, a 1967 bequest of land to the county prompted the adoption of a formal Park and Open Space Plan in 1972. One of the first acquisitions under the new plan was the abandoned Bloomer Nursery in Clinton Township. Today this 79-acre site serves as the county arboretum, and is unique in having whole mature groves of a single kind of tree or shrub—stands of oaks, birches, or weeping cherry—creating a horticultural "zoo." A reproduction 1893 gazebo with brick terrace, a wetland study area with boardwalk trail, and display gardens of annuals and perennials are some of the highlights of the arboretum, which also serves as headquarters for the Hunterdon County Park System.

Hunterdon County Arboretum, Clinton Township, Hunterdon County

$\mathcal{B}$rookdale Farm was the name of the Thompson estate in Lincroft, where William Payne Thompson built his mansion in 1893. It remained the family estate until the death of philanthropist Geraldine Thompson in 1967, who bequeathed the 215-acre estate to the county. Today, Thompson Park serves as headquarters for the Monmouth County Park System. To the east of the mansion lies a rose garden named in memory of the dean of American commercial rosarians, Lambertus C. Bobbink. This fountain-centered garden, famous for its aromatic display of blossoms that bloom from May through October, is an official All-American Rose

*B*arclay Farmstead traces its origins to 1684 when it was settled by a Quaker, John Kay. The farm's Federal-style brick house was built in the 1820s by the second owner, Joseph Thorn. The Joseph W. Cooper family owned the property for the next century and a half, before Cooper's descendant, Helen Champion Barclay, sold it to the Township of Cherry Hill in 1974. The grounds reflect a typical South Jersey Quaker farm with a fine herb garden near the kitchen and an apple orchard. Part of the 32-acre grounds are farmed today through a yearly rental program to community residents. The farmstead is owned and operated by the Township of Cherry Hill, and its restoration efforts are also aided by the Friends of Barclay Farmstead.

Barclay Farmstead, Cherry Hill, Camden County

*N*ear the highway corridors of the New Jersey Turnpike and Routes 1 and 18 lies a lush garden haven. The Rutgers Display Gardens, established in 1921, integrates teaching, research, and public outreach through the Rutgers Cooperative Extension Service. Home of the world's largest collection of American hollies, Rutgers Gardens also boasts fine collections of dogwoods, flowering shrubs, and ornamentals. The Donald B. Lacey Annual Garden serves as a demonstration garden for the New Jersey home gardener in selecting successful annual flowers. As a facility of Cook College of Rutgers University, the gardens are also supported by the Friends of Rutgers Gardens through contributions and hands-on volunteerism.

amed in honor of the beloved Sister Mary Grace, department chairperson and professor of biology from 1927 to 1968, the arboretum at Georgian Court College is the 150-acre preservation of the original gardens of the Gould estate. Originally planned as a winter home, George Jay Gould purchased the land in 1896 and hired the services of the famous New York architect Bruce Price to transform the grounds into a lavish English country estate of the Georgian period; thus the estate was named Georgian Court. Price designed three of the four major gardens: the Classic Italian Garden, the Sunken Garden and Lagoon, and the Formal Garden near the mansion, with its maze-like paths. Gould later added a Japanese Garden, hiring the noted designer Takeo Shiota. After Gould's death in 1923, the Sisters of Mercy of North Plainfield bought the estate the following year and created Georgian Court College.

Sister Mary Grace Burns Arboretum at Georgian Court College ● Lakewood, Ocean County

Coastal research and education are the primary concerns of the Wetlands Institute in Stone Harbor. Located on 6,000 acres of magnificent salt marshes and tidal creeks, the Wetlands Institute provides an elevated boardwalk and nature trails for enhanced viewing of the abundant flora and fauna. Near the gray cedar-shake headquarters building are found colorful flower gardens that feature a spring and summer array of annuals and perennials. They were recently dedicated as "Marion's Garden" in honor of the garden's creator and steadfast caretaker, Marion Glaspey. The formal plantings are in vivid contrast to the endless expanse of green marsh grass and blue water.

*E*migrating from Ireland in 1704, Michael Kearny settled in Perth Amboy in the early 18th century. The Kearny Cottage, constructed in 1781, remained as the family homestead of this prominent military and political family for almost a century and a half. When threatened with its destruction in the 1920s, concerned citizens campaigned for its preservation and subsequent "moves" within Perth Amboy. At its present site, the historic cottage is complemented by a raised-bed herb and perennial garden, which contains exotic plants that reflect Commodore Lawrence Kearny's world travels. A unique collection of carriage "stepping stones" also adds interest to the garden. Kearny Cottage is owned by the city of Perth Amboy and is cared for by the Kearny Cottage Historical Society.

*W*arinanco Park in Roselle features a colorful flower garden which was created in 1936, and later named in honor of one of the original commissioners of the Union County Park Commission, Henry S. Chatfield. Each spring this compact garden is transformed into a sea of vivid color, thanks to the planting of over 14,000 tulips; nearby, in the park, azaleas, magnolias, and Japanese cherry trees complete the scene. In summer the tulips are replaced by almost 10,000 annuals, which provide continuous color until the first frost. Maintained by the Union County Department of Parks and Recreation, Chatfield Garden's circular design, intersecting paths, and benches for enjoying the view create a tranquil respite within the park.

Henry S. Chatfield Memorial Garden at Warinanco Park, Roselle, Union County

Inventor Thomas Alva Edison, widowed in 1884, found new love in Mina Miller, and in 1886 purchased a mansion for his bride-to-be on the mountain-side of West Orange, in an area known as Llewellyn Park. This estate, with its 23-room Victorian home on over 13 acres, became known as Glenmont, and remained as Edison's home until his death in 1931. Edison purchased the home from Henry C. Pedder, a New York businessman who hired architect Henry Hudson Holly to design the home and grounds. The Edisons enjoyed horticulture and maintained a full-time staff to care for the many exotic specimen trees and shrubs, flower gardens, fruit trees, expansive lawns, and greenhouse. Today, Glenmont and Edison's Laboratory are national museums under the supervision of the National Park Service at West Orange.

A t the entrance to Taylor Park in downtown Millburn, visitors pass through the beautiful Wallbridge Rose Garden, named in honor of Mrs. William Wallbridge, garden club enthusiast and friend of the park's founder, Mrs. Taylor. The Wallbridge estate bequeathed funds to restore the original garden at Taylor Park. The Short Hills Garden Club created the rose garden in 1981, and continues to care for it in cooperation with the Millburn Parks Commission. The garden is based around a central gazebo, and features hundreds of rose plants, arranged in concentric rings in four triangular beds. Besides the rose specialty, the garden also offers plantings of Korean boxwood, azaleas, rhododendrons, sorrel trees, and holly to provide visual appeal throughout the year.

Wallbridge Rose Garden, Millburn, Essex County

*W*hippany Farm was the name given to the summer estate of George G. Frelinghuysen, who built his stately Colonial Revival mansion there in 1891. His daughter, Mathilda, inherited the property and participated in the plans to convert her private estate into a public arboretum by generously donating the 127-acre tract to the people of Morris County in 1969. Serving as headquarters for the Morris County Park Commission, Frelinghuysen Arboretum is known for its rose garden and lilac garden, flowering trees and shrubs, and a varied assortment of other specialized plantings, trails, and collections—many acquired through the generosity of private donors and volunteer organizations.

George Griswold Frelinghuysen Arboretum, Morristown, Morris County

George Griswold Frelinghuysen Arboretum, Morristown, Morris County

*C*urrently, Bamboo Brook serves as an Outdoor Education Center for the Morris County Park Commission. Originally known as Merchiston Farm, it was also the home of William and Martha Brookes Hutcheson from 1911 through 1959, and was donated to the county in their memory in 1974. In the late 1920s Mrs. Hutcheson, a noted landscape architect, designed the five-acre formal garden that surrounds the house. Water features and mature native specimen trees highlight the formal and naturalistic plantings found at Bamboo Brook. Stone walls and steps line the trails that lead to the fields, forest, and brook of this 100-acre "Highlands" retreat.

$\mathcal{R}$ ock outcroppings of the Palisades complement a Japanese Garden on the corporate campus of Prentice-Hall Publishing Company in Englewood Cliffs. Begun in 1960 when Constance Powers presented her son, Prentice-Hall president John G. Powers, a gift of a stone Japanese lantern, the garden was created to commemorate Japanese–American cultural relations. With the acquisition of more stone lanterns, statuary, and a replica of a traditional Japanese wooden bridge which crosses a small stream, the Japanese Garden was complete and now serves as a peaceful respite for the employees of Prentice-Hall.

Prentice-Hall Japanese Garden, Englewood Cliffs, Bergen County

*N*amed for its freshwater spring, Cold Spring was a popular stop on the stage coach route from Philadelphia to Cape May. Today, Historic Cold Spring Village is a collection of 18th- and 19th-century buildings from Cape May County that recreates the atmosphere of a typical "Down Jersey" farm community of the 1840s. Many of the structures are enhanced by special plantings of flower gardens, vegetable gardens, herb gardens, and farm fields. The living history village was founded in 1973 by Dr. Joseph Salvatore and was opened to the public in 1981. The Salvatores later donated the land and buildings to Cape May County for continued historic preservation and park purposes.

Historic Cold Spring Village Gardens, Cold Spring, Cape May County

$\mathcal{L}$eaming's Run is a small brook named after Thomas Leaming, a whaler who first settled this site in Cape May County in the late 1600s. The Leaming house, which was built in 1706, is the only remaining house of New Jersey's whaling days. The current owners, the Aprill family, moved to Swainton in 1959 and began developing a world-class botanical garden consisting of 27 different thematic areas around Leaming's Run, which flows through the property. With names like Reflecting Garden, Ferny Vista, Down Jersey Country Garden, and Bridal Garden, Leaming's Run Botanical Gardens covers over 20 acres with flowers, ferns, lawns, and ponds.

Blooms of annuals provide continuous color from May through October, and many of the gardens are dedicated to flowers of a single color. In August, hundreds of hummingbirds are attracted to the gardens, making it a special place to view these colorful birds. There is also a replica Colonial farm that depicts early whaling life in New Jersey and contains gardens and crops from the time of Thomas Leaming. All of these gardens are found along a mile-long looping path that offers an easy and delightful walk through a botanical paradise.

Leaming's Run Botanical Gardens, Swainton, Cape May County

At the Johnson Ferry House in Washington Crossing State Park, the gardens are undergoing a transformation from the existing Colonial Revival gardens, established by the Daughters of the American Revolution in 1926, into a sampler reproduction of an 18th-century Dutch kitchen garden, which more closely represents the gardens planted by its original inhabitants from the Netherlands. Herbs have been interplanted with old variety perennials, and a new emphasis has been placed on European vegetables, small fruits, flax, and dye plants. On the other side of the house, a small garden of spring perennials welcomes visitors to its door.

Ferry House Kitchen Garden, Washington Crossing, Mercer County

*W*hen Uriah (Yurrie) Van Riper married Maria (Polly) Berdan in 1786, he built her a
Dutch-style stone farmhouse in the hills of Wayne, New Jersey. The house was passed
down to their great-granddaughter Mary Ann Van Riper, who married Andrew Hopper
in 1872. The Van Ripers and the Hoppers continued to occupy the house for almost two centuries,
until Wayne Township acquired the property in 1964 and created a museum which was opened
to the public eight years later. Situated beside the Point View Reservoir, the museum's parklike
grounds contain mature trees and shrubs, flower beds, and a beautiful Colonial herb garden
which is cared for by the Pine Lake Garden Club.

*O*riginally part of a Colonial farm, John H. Wisner built his house on this property in 1889 and commissioned Calvert Vaux, a partner of Frederick Law Olmsted, to draft a landscape plan for the grounds. The Wisners were the first to plant daffodils on the site. In 1916 the Reeves family bought the estate and hired Ellen Shipman, a renowned landscape architect, to continue with an overall plan. The Reed family became the third owners in the 1960s and added the herb garden and woodland trails. April begins the season with thousands of daffodils blooming in a natural glacial bowl just behind the mansion, while nearby azaleas, rhododendrons, roses, daylilies, and perennials continue the ever-changing progression into summer. The arboretum is owned by the city of Summit and is maintained and supported solely through memberships, contributions, and volunteerism.

$\mathcal{C}$ ape May's Victorian heritage is elegantly displayed at the Emlen Physick Estate, an 1879 Stick-style mansion, designed by the renowned architect Frank Furness. Dr. Emlen Physick was heir to a wealthy Philadelphia family, and lived the life of a Victorian country gentleman here until 1916. After a series of subsequent owners, the estate fell into terrible decline and was saved from destruction in 1970 by the formation of the Mid-Atlantic Center for the Arts. Contributions and countless volunteer hours saved the house and gardens, restoring them to their former grandeur. Based on original photographs, the grounds appeared rustic, and current garden restoration efforts reflect the 1880s with period plantings of annuals, perennials, trees, and shrubs.

Emlen Physick Estate, Cape May, Cape May County

William Shakespeare incorporated numerous flower and plant references into his writings. In 1927, on the 363rd anniversary of his birth, two Plainfield organizations, The Shakespeare Society and the Plainfield Garden Club, followed a tradition started at Stratford-on-Avon in England, by creating a garden in his honor at Cedarbrook Park. Over 40 flowers and plants mentioned in Shakespeare's plays and sonnets are planted throughout its 17 geometrically designed flower beds and borders. The garden, complete with sundial and pergola, was designed by Olmsted Brothers, internationally renowned landscape architects, and is maintained today by the Union County Park Commission in cooperation with the Plainfield Garden Club.

Shakespeare Garden at Cedarbrook Park, Plainfield, Union County

*E*vert Van Wickle arrived in New Amsterdam in 1664 and settled in New Lotts, Long Island, in 1686. As a successful carpenter, Van Wickle later speculated in the purchase of 1,250 acres of land along the Raritan River in New Jersey. In 1722 his youngest son, Symen, moved to his father's land and built his house two miles north of the busy town called Raritan Landing. Numerous owners have occupied the house since Symen Van Wickle, the latest being The Meadows Foundation, which in 1976 purchased the property for preservation and restoration. Today the property known as The Meadows also contains a nature trail, canal bridge, and the Reinmann Memorial Garden, a formal wedding garden which is maintained by volunteers of The Meadows Foundation.

Van Wickle House Garden, Franklin Township, Somerset County

*N*estled in the Hacklebarney Hills, Willowwood began as an 18th-century farm. It was
purchased in 1908 by Henry and Robert Tubbs, whose hobby of collecting and growing
distinctive plants lasted for more than a half-century. These horticulturists transformed
the farmland into an arboretum containing about 3,500 kinds of native and exotic plants, including
a rare Dawn Redwood tree, now more than 70 feet high. Named for its collection of 110 different
willows, the arboretum also boasts fine collections of oaks, maples, cherries, conifers, lilacs, and
magnolias—perhaps New Jersey's finest collection of temperate-zoned "Piedmont" flora.

Willowwood Arboretum, Chester Township, Morris County

Willowwood Arboretum, Chester Township, Morris County

173

Two formal gardens, the Cottage Garden and Pan's Garden, complement the 1783 residence and 1790s stone barn, as numerous informal paths traverse the remaining 130 acres of meadow, marsh, and woodland, leading to delightful areas with names like Treasure Trove, Bee Meadow, Elephant Walk, and Buttonwood Hollow. Willowwood was established as a private arboretum in 1950, with the proprietorship being passed on to Rutgers University from 1967 to 1980. It was then acquired by the Morris County Park Commission which currently maintains the arboretum with support from various volunteer organizations.

Willowwood Arboretum, Chester Township, Morris County

*D*esigned and developed during the 1970s by Rudolf W. van der Goot, Somerset County Park Commission's first horticulturist, the rose gardens were renamed in his honor in 1981. The formal gardens reflect the original designs of the Mettler Estate and are divided into three formal areas, the Mettler Garden, Central Garden, and Dutch Garden. These gardens feature 4,000 plants, comprising 275 varieties of modern and old-fashioned roses of all types. The garden is also an accredited All-American Rose Selections Garden, displaying the current year's winners. As part of the Colonial Park Arboretum, the rose garden is maintained by the Somerset County Park Commission.

Rudolf W. van der Goot Rose Garden, Colonial Park Arboretum, Franklin Township, Somerset County

$\mathcal{A}$s part of the Colonial Park Arboretum, the Somerset County Park Commission, with generous assistance from the Franklin Township Lions Club, developed a wheelchair-accessible, braille-labeled "garden for the senses" in 1981. A brick path through the Rudolf van der Goot Rose Garden leads to this sensory garden which features annuals, perennials, and herbs with interesting textures and wonderful scents. The plants selected for the Fragrance and Sensory Garden are meant to be touched, sniffed, and tasted, as well as seen. Completely renovated in 1989, the garden's rock walls, circular path, and areas to sit and reflect create a welcome setting for all visitors.

Fragrance and Sensory Garden, Colonial Park Arboretum, Franklin Township, Somerset County

Fragrance and Sensory Garden at Colonial Park Arboretum, Franklin Township, Somerset County

EPILOGUE

By

Walter Choroszewski

Gardens have played an important part in my life. At a very early age I shared in my parents' enthusiasm for gardening.

My father, a coal miner by trade, was really a farmer at heart—growing a wide array of vegetables in his backyard garden. The short growing season in the mountains of Pennsylvania was always a challenge to him. Risking a late spring frost, he would often plant very early in hopes of extending the growing season. I especially remember one year, with a successful March planting to his credit, when he watched as his prized garden was decimated by a June hailstorm. My mother told him that he was getting too proud of his early success, and that "The Lord had given, and the Lord had taken away." With a new perspective, he turned over the soil, and started planting all over again.

With pitchfork, watering can, or wheelbarrow, my father was always at work in his garden. Early ripe tomatoes, cucumbers, string beans, and peppers were shared with the neighbors. The later harvest produced onions, potatoes, cabbages, and gigantic pumpkins that looked like orange mountains on the garden's horizon.

The challenge of the weeds was my mother's mission, as she often left small piles of the unwanted grasses and weeds all along the garden beds. My father appreciated the help, but complained bitterly about this "hit-and-run" approach, as he was the one to clean up and cart away the weeds.

My mother's garden favorites were her flowers. A smaller garden area was dedicated to flowers and it provided us with constant color, from the purples of spring through the pinks and reds of summer, to the yellows and golds of early autumn—irises, lilacs, lupines, peonies, roses, pansies, geraniums, gladioluses, zinnias, strawflowers, and chrysanthemums. She would often bring the cut flowers indoors; when the deep purple French lilacs would bloom, the sweet aroma was everywhere as bouquets were placed in almost every room of the house.

Fruit trees were present throughout our property—apple trees grew in the front yard, and pear trees dominated the vegetable garden, with token peach and plum trees scattered between. A lush grapevine comprised of white Tokay and Concord grapes was the focal point of the back yard. Many of these were planted by my maternal grandfather, who taught my father the art of grafting and caring for this mini-orchard. The frost that we feared in spring was welcomed in fall; it added a magical sweetness to the grapes before they were picked.

The fruitful bounty was then transformed into pies, cakes, jellies, and wine. The canning of the peaches and pears was also an important part of the harvest, along with the preserving of other garden vegetables—tomatoes, peppers, dill pickles, "bread & butter" pickles, red beets, relish, and "chow-chow." I remember well my parents' hard work dedicated to this process, and I can still hear the sounds of mason jar lids "popping" in the night, as they cooled on our kitchen table.

As an adult I can't seem to find as much time for my own garden as my parents once found for theirs. The Choroszewski family garden today consists of a wildflower field, a vegetable garden, beds of spring bulbs, annuals, and perennials, some flowering shrubs, and a few scattered trees. After the spring planting and some minimal maintenance, our garden is entrusted to nature's care, which usually provides us with very pleasing results.

I am grateful for the people who do find the time to care for the many public gardens throughout New Jersey. Often these gardens are maintained by volunteer-based organizations or garden clubs whose members personally donate plant materials and valuable time to beautify our state. Other gardens are staffed by expert horticulturists who showcase their talents in magnificent estate gardens, parks, or arboretums.

I find pleasure in the beauty of a well-maintained garden, and I often stopped at these fine gardens while on my photographic sojourns throughout New Jersey. Visiting and photographing these gardens gave me the inspiration for this book.

Often I was alone in these gardens, as I visited them during the early hours of dawn or just before dusk, seeking a warm, low-angled light. Other times I waited for an overcast day, to photograph the range of color in a shadowless, even light.

This book was not designed to be a complete guidebook, as many beautiful gardens were not included. Instead, it is presented as a personal tour of some of my favorite garden locations within New Jersey. I chose not to provide horticultural information as my goal was to share the total garden environment that I found in my travels.

A garden provides us with many lessons of life, and it gives us a greater appreciation of the wonders of nature—the rhythm of the seasons, and the simple gifts of sunshine and rain.

SOURCES

In writing my text for each garden, I obtained information by personal interview or through supplied literature from the respective gardens. Unfortunately, I am not able to credit the original authors of the brochures, press releases, book references, and newspaper articles that were made available to me; however, I am very appreciative of their invaluable contribution as an indirect source for this project. Other reading sources for information included:

Bishop, Gordon. *Gems of New Jersey*, written for the *Star-Ledger*. Englewood Cliffs, N.J.: Prentice-Hall, Inc., 1985.

Cunningham, John T. *New Jersey, America's Main Road*. Andover, N.J.: Afton Publishing Company, 1976.

Cunningham, John T. *The New Jersey Sampler, Historic Tales of Old New Jersey*. Florham Park, N.J.: Afton Publishing Company, 1977.

Miller, Everitt L., and Cohen, Dr. Jay S. *The American Garden Guidebook*. New York: M. Evans and Company, Inc., 1987.

Mulligan, William C. *The Complete Guide to North American Gardens, The Northeast*. Boston: Little Brown and Company, 1991.

Quiller-Couch, Sir Arthur. *The Oxford Book of English Verse, 1250–1918*. Oxford, England: Clarendon Press, 1955.

Toth, Edwin J. *New Jersey Directory of Gardens and Horticultural Destinations*. Far Hills, N.J.: Somerset County Park Commission, Horticulture Department, 1985.

ACKNOWLEDGMENTS

I would like to thank the respective owners of all the gardens, who graciously allowed me to photograph and share the beauty of their gardens in this book. And although I couldn't mention each individually, all were most hospitable, enthusiastic, and cooperative in supplying information for the text.

Personal and professional friends have been helpful and supportive throughout this long project. I've asked for their creative input, opinions on color or style, expertise on grammar, punctuation, or vocabulary, and help with proofreading—thank you one and all.

Regarding the production, I am sincerely indebted to Sherrie Bach, who persevered in contacting all of the gardens, and provided countless hours in assembling the mechanicals and bringing order to the chaos. I am also especially grateful for the important contacts that were provided to me by Suzanne Poor.

Unlike my previous efforts, this book offers a text which presented a greater challenge than just simple caption writing. I am truly grateful for the contributions of Mary Martis and her staff—Perry Del Purgatorio, Kevin Gilligan, and Mary Fitzgerald—and for their typographical and proofreading expertise.

The words of an old friend, John T. Cunningham, have graced the introductions of my books since 1981, and I am honored and pleased to present his insightful contribution to this book. Thanks, John!

Most importantly, I am grateful for the patience, love, and support of my family—my son, Joe, whose musical talents kept me company during writing and editing, and whose sharp-eyed proofreading skills helped greatly in the eleventh hour; and my wife, Susan, whose creative ideas and valued opinions are planted throughout this book, and whose total input to this project cannot possibly be measured or properly credited. Thank you!

DIRECTORY

ACORN HALL GARDENS
Morris County Historical Society Headquarters
68 Morris Avenue
Morristown, Morris County
201 267-3465

BAMBOO BROOK
Longview Road
Chester Township, Morris County
201 326-7600

BARCLAY FARMSTEAD
209 Barclay Lane
Cherry Hill, Camden County
609 795-6225

BRANCH BROOK PARK
Clifton Avenue
Newark, Essex County
and
Mill Street
Belleville, Essex County
201 857-8530

BROOKDALE PARK ROSE GARDEN
Brookdale Park
Grove & Montclair Streets
Bloomfield, Essex County
201 857-8530

BUCCLEUCH MANSION GARDENS
Easton Avenue
New Brunswick, Middlesex County
908 745-5112

CANNONBALL MUSEUM GARDEN
East Front Street
Scotch Plains, Union County
908 322-6700

CORA HARTSHORN ARBORETUM
324 Forest Drive South
Short Hills, Essex County
201 376-3587

CRANE HOUSE MUSEUM GARDEN
110 Orange Road
Montclair, Essex County
201 744-1796

CROSS ESTATE GARDEN
Old Jockey Hollow Road
Bernardsville, Somerset County
201 539-2016

DEEP CUT GARDENS
Deep Cut Park
352 Redhill Road
Middletown, Monmouth County
908 671-6050

DEY MANSION GARDENS
199 Totowa Road
Wayne, Passaic County
201 696-1776

DRUMTHWACKET
354 Stockton Street
Princeton, Mercer County
609 683-0057

DUKE GARDENS
Route 206 South
Hillsborough Township, Somerset County
908 722-3700

EAST JERSEY OLDE TOWNE HERB GARDEN
Johnson Park
River Road
Piscataway, Middlesex County
908 745-4489

EDITH DUFF GWINN MEMORIAL GARDEN
Central Avenue & 5th Street
Barnegat Light, Ocean County
609 494-3522

EMLEN PHYSICK ESTATE
1048 Washington Street
Cape May, Cape May County
609 884-5404

ERLANGER MEMORIAL GARDENS at
MONMOUTH COLLEGE
West Cedar Avenue
West Long Branch, Monmouth County
908 571-3400

FERRY HOUSE KITCHEN GARDEN
Washington Crossing State Park
355 Washington Crossing Penn Road
Washington Crossing, Mercer County
609 737-2515

FLORENCE AND ROBERT ZUCK ARBORETUM at
DREW UNIVERSITY
Madison Avenue
Madison, Morris County
201 408-3358

FRAGRANCE AND SENSORY GARDEN at
COLONIAL PARK ARBORETUM
Colonial Park - Parking Lot A
Mettlers Road
Franklin Township, Somerset County
908 873-2459

GARDEN FOR THE BLIND AND
PHYSICALLY HANDICAPPED
Iselin Library
1081 Green Street
Iselin, Middlesex County
908 283-1200

GEORGE GRISWOLD FRELINGHUYSEN ARBORETUM
53 East Hanover Avenue
Morris Township, Morris County
201 326-7600

GEORGE WASHINGTON MEMORIAL ARBORETUM
Washington Crossing State Park
355 Washington Crossing Penn Road
Washington Crossing, Mercer County
609 737-0623

GLENMONT
Edison National Historic Site
Main Street & Lakeside
Llewellyn Park
West Orange, Essex County
201 736-0550

HELEN C. BRANSON HERB GARDEN
Greenfield Hall
343 Kings Highway East
Haddonfield, Camden County
609 429-7375

HENRY S. CHATFIELD MEMORIAL GARDEN at
WARINANCO PARK
Jersey Avenue
Elizabeth, Union County
908 527-4824

HEREFORD INLET LIGHTHOUSE GARDEN
1st Street & Central Avenue
North Wildwood, Cape May County
609 522-4520

HISTORIC COLD SPRING VILLAGE GARDENS
Route 9 or Route 626
Cold Spring, Cape May County
609 898-2300

HOLMDEL ARBORETUM
Holmdel Park
Longstreet Road
Holmdel Township, Monmouth County
908 431-7903

HUNTERDON COUNTY ARBORETUM
Route 31
Clinton Township, Hunterdon County
908 782-1158

KEARNY COTTAGE GARDEN
63 Catalpa Avenue
Perth Amboy, Middlesex County
908 826-1826

KUSER FARM MANSION GARDENS
390 Newkirk Avenue
Hamilton Township, Mercer County
609 890-3630

LAMBERTUS C. BOBBINK
MEMORIAL ROSE GARDEN
Thompson Park
Newman Springs Road
Lincroft, Monmouth County
908 842-4000

LEAMINGS RUN BOTANICAL GARDENS
1845 Route 9
Swainton, Cape May County
609 465-5871

LEONARD J. BUCK GARDENS
11 Layton Road
Far Hills, Somerset County
908 234-2677

LONGSTREET FARM
Holmdel Park
Longstreet Road
Holmdel Township, Monmouth County
908 946-3758

MACCULLOCH HALL GARDENS
45 Macculloch Avenue
Morristown, Morris County
201 538-2404

MARQUAND PARK
Lovers Lane
Princeton, Mercer County
609 497-7629

MILLBROOK VILLAGE GARDEN
Delaware Water Gap National Recreation Area
Millbrook, Warren County
717 588-2432

MILLER-CORY HOUSE GARDENS
614 Mountain Avenue
Westfield, Union County
908 232-1776

NEW JERSEY STATE BOTANICAL GARDENS at SKYLANDS
Ringwood State Park
Skylands Manor Section
Ringwood, Passaic County
201 962-7031

NEW JERSEY STATE CAPITOL COMPLEX GARDENS
The State House
West State Street
Trenton, Mercer County
609 292-4661

PHOENIX HOUSE GARDEN
Mendham Municipal Building
2 West Main Street
Mendham, Morris County
201 543-7152

PRENTICE-HALL JAPANESE GARDEN
Prentice-Hall Building
113 Sylvan Avenue (Route 9W)
Englewood Cliffs, Bergen County
201 592-2000

PRESBY MEMORIAL IRIS GARDEN
474 Upper Mountain Avenue
Upper Montclair, Essex County
201 783-5974

PROSPECT GARDENS at PRINCETON UNIVERSITY
Washington Road
Princeton, Mercer County
609 258-3455

REEVES-REED ARBORETUM
165 Hobart Avenue
Summit, Union County
908 273-8787

RINGWOOD MANOR GARDENS
Ringwood State Park
Ringwood Manor Section
Ringwood, Passaic County
201 962-7031

ROCKINGHAM HERB GARDEN
Route 518 (East of Rocky Hill)
Franklin Township, Somerset County
609 921-8835

RUDOLF W. VAN DER GOOT ROSE GARDEN
Colonial Park - Parking Lot A
Mettlers Road
Franklin Township, Somerset County
908 873-2459

RUTGERS DISPLAY GARDENS
Rutgers University - Cook College
Ryders Lane
New Brunswick, Middlesex County
908 932-9271

SHAKESPEARE GARDEN at
CEDARBROOK PARK
Park Avenue
Plainfield, Union County
908 527-4900

SHAKESPEARE GARDEN at
COLLEGE OF ST. ELIZABETH
2 Convent Road
Convent Station, Morris County
201 292-6327

SISTER MARY GRACE BURNS ARBORETUM at
GEORGIAN COURT COLLEGE
900 Lakewood Avenue
Lakewood, Ocean County
908 364-2200

SMITHVILLE MANSION COURTYARD GARDENS
Burlington County Park
Smithville Road
Eastampton Township, Burlington County
609 265-5068

TRENT HOUSE HERB GARDEN
15 Market Street
Trenton, Mercer County
609 989-3027

VAN RIPER-HOPPER HOUSE
533 Berdan Avenue
Wayne, Passaic County
201 694-7192

VAN WICKLE HOUSE GARDEN
1289 Easton Avenue
Franklin Township, Somerset County
908 828-7418

WALLBRIDGE ROSE GARDEN
Taylor Park
Millburn Avenue
Millburn, Essex County
201 564-7058

WASHINGTON SPRING GARDEN at VAN SAUN PARK
Forest Avenue
Paramus, Bergen County
201 646-2680

WATERLOO VILLAGE HERB GARDEN
Waterloo Village
Waterloo Road
Byram, Sussex County
201 347-0900

WELL-SWEEP HERB FARM
317 Mount Bethel Road
Port Murray, Warren County
908 852-5390

WETLANDS INSTITUTE GARDEN
1075 Stone Harbor Road
Stone Harbor, Cape May County
609 368-1211

WICK HOUSE KITCHEN GARDEN
Morristown National Historic Park
Jockey Hollow Section
Tempe Wick Road
Harding Township, Morris County
201 539-2016

WILLOWWOOD ARBORETUM
Longview Road
Chester Township, Morris County
908 234-0992

INDEX